(I) Read it.

Thought you might appreciate

at least parts of it —

much

love

Jim.

Living,

Loving,

&

Leaving

Living,

Loving,

&

Leaving

JOHN RAPOZA

photographs by
Rodrick S. Schubert

Gibbs Associates
Boulder, Colorado

This book is typeset in Carter & Cone Galliard.
All text pages and cover were composited using Quark XPress.
Photographs were scanned from transparencies or negatives
using the Kodak ProPhotoCD System.
The images were then processed using
Adobe PhotoShop to create duotone image files.
Films used were Agfa Scala 200x, Ilford XP2 Super, and Ilford HP5.
(All names are property of their respective owners.)

Designed and typeset in the United States by Shoestring Graphics
Printed and bound in Singapore by CS Graphics

Contents

LEAVING

FORWARD

Poetry has always been a means for expressing my
emotions. Whenever I felt an emotion that persisted I
would start writing poetry. Sometimes the emotions would
come unexpectedly. One poem topic was suggested by a
friend while hiking and by the end of the hike the poem
was completed *(Aspen in Autumn)*. Another poem
materialized while I was walking by a cemetery *(Eternal
Gardens)*. I had no pen or paper with me so I rushed into a
nearby bank and used one of the dangling pens and the
back of a brochure to write down the poem before I forgot
the lines. I don't follow all the rules in poetry writing, I feel
it is the image that is important. (It's called poetic license.)

In reviewing my poetry I found that it primarily fell into
three major categories. The first was about life and living,
the second about love and loving and the third about
leaving, a prospect we must all face someday.

My hope is that as you read these poems you too may
become more aware of feelings and emotions within
yourself and others. May the reading bring you a great deal
of pleasure.

— *John Rapoza*
Boulder, Colorado

BIOGRAPHY

John Rapoza was born in New England (Fall River, Massachusetts) and lived in California and Pennsylvania before settling in Boulder, Colorado.

His academic background is in engineering (University of Massachusetts at Dartmouth) and Industrial Psychology (California State University at Northridge). He is now retired. John took care of his wife at home for twelve years before she succumbed to Alzheimer's disease in 1999. He has been a volunteer speaker for the Alzheimer's Association and enjoys hiking, cycling, skiing, travelling, and writing. John has three children and two grandchildren all living in California. He has written many articles for *Care Connections,* a caregivers publication distributed by Community Services of Boulder County.

Five of his poems were published in the 75TH anniversary publication of the Colorado Poetry Society.

DEDICATION

To my late wife Dorothy whose courage and determination during the last phases of her life while battling Alzheimer's disease forced me to re-evaluate my own priorities in life and inspired some of the poems in the Leaving section of this book.

Also to my three children; Daryl, John, and Russell who have been a stimulus to my writing and whose exemplary lives would make any dad proud.

Living

ASPEN IN AUTUMN

New England born I often scoffed
At the Aspen fables I'm told
Where the leaves are only one color
As they turn from yellow to gold

I remember the oaks and the walnuts
And the other hard woods that I've known
Where nature has tinted its dying leaves
Into bright reds, yellows and browns

Where the trees stretch up to the heavens
And the leaves lay a carpet so grand
Where they come from all over the world
To witness this beautiful land

I've now come to enjoy the real beauty of life
Where the Aspen are always in sight
Where Colorado performs its magic
As the leaves flutter toward the light

This year I'll not be traveling East
Where the leaves are brightest I'm told
I'll walk along the trails I love
Where the leaves turn from yellow to gold

FOURTH *of* JULY

Fondest of memories, echoes from the past
Music of yesteryear, sounds that always last
The pavilion still stands of sturdy oak wood
Notches in the rail where the tuba once stood

Sunday afternoons when the people all came
Bringing with them sunshine, will it ever be the same
Laughter of the children stilled by music's charm
Eyes aglow with wonder holding onto Mom

Lovers holding hands pressing face to face
Hoping no one notices their intimate embrace
Elders sitting quietly on wood folding chairs
Dreaming of days gone by, when the world was theirs

The bandmaster stood proudly waving his baton
The brassy sound of music where has it all gone
I loved the stirring marches, the best we could command
Never mind the fireworks, let's bring back the band

THE WEAVER

The sounds of the loom can be heard by all
By those who listen with mind alert
The warp and woof of daily toil
Some of whom feel, some of whom hurt

Ask not why we who are labor bound
By tasks that seem to burden so
The load is lighter so we have found
From the faces of those we hold

The weaver works not for trophies and fame
But looks beyond daily struggles and strife
To where sounds of music and beauty reign
And weaves the fabric of life

COLORADO SKIES

Among the wonders of the world
And all the treasures prompting sighs
We must pause to add another
It's those Colorado skies

They come down from the heavens
And surround the mountains high
To caress the snow capped peaks
With those Colorado skies

Early morning brings its beauty
With the brightness of the sun
As the cotton clouds abound us
And God's landscape has begun
Oh the colors leave you breathless
As the sun begins to set
And nature's glory comes before you
Painting hues you can't forget

And as darkness overwhelms us
To allow the stars to shine
They seem close enough to pluck them
From those Colorado skies

You can praise the sunny beaches
And the mountain streams on high
Let me stretch up toward the heavens
And touch those Colorado skies

I REMEMBER

I remember walking on them
Those paths along the shore
Looking out toward the ocean
With its never ending roar

How refreshing in the morning
With cool breezes overhead
As the seagulls plucked their breakfast
From the ocean's banquet spread

I recall the tranquil feeling
With my feet beneath the waves
As I pondered life's long memories
Taking much more than I gave

Though the burdens of the world
Rest on your shoulders high
Nothing soothes the troubled soul
As the ocean's foaming tides

As the scent of ocean currents
Takes you back along the years
With the many friends you met there
Sharing laughter, sharing tears

Yes, I remember walking on them
Those paths along the shore
As I looked out toward the ocean
With its never-ending roar

EMOTIONS

Emotions are the stream of life
They keep the juices flowing
They push us here and push us there
Without our even knowing

Some are good and some are bad
They're felt from Oxnard to Bangor
And most destructive of them all
Are jealousy and anger

THE BEACH

I want to go to the beach today
Where the sun is warm and bright
Where the sand is covered with seaweed
And the children all shout with delight

I want to go to the beach today
Where there's no one to set my pace
Where the sound of waves is relaxing
And the kids kick sand in your face

For there's a time and place to be busy
And a time and place to rest
I want to go to the beach today
Where loafing is at its best

I need to hear that sound again
Of seagulls on the beach
I need to see that sight again
Of waves within my reach

I need to feel that warmth again
Of sand upon my back
Of cooling breezes overhead
And sailboats as they tack

I need to watch the sunset
Fall slowly out of sight
As darkness blankets the horizon
And daylight turns to night

LEARN TO LIVE

When you awake each bright new day
Take a deep breath, refresh your soul
Look forward to your arising
Let accomplishment be your goal

Be alert to those around you
They are your companions on your journey
Their needs are not unlike your own
And no less worthy

It is now with time we must regard
With thought and contemplation should enjoy
And each remaining moment jealously guard
To savor those treasures with all we can employ

Enjoy this day as if it were your last
There is beauty everywhere
Be not hurried to reach your end
There'll be enough time there

To the west the hues of which we are so fond
We with others the wide horizon share
Wait not until you go beyond
There are no sunsets there

MEDITATION

Too long I've lived the city life
Where traffic and crime abound
It's time to take another look
At other places I've found

Too short this life we all know well
And the choices that have to be made
To live, to play, to gather wealth
For too soon they too must fade

Don't bother ever to find out why
There is no rhyme or reason
When the time comes you will be there
Whenever the day or season

Take a hike along the way
Where the trail just winds and weaves
And walk until the sun goes down
On a cushion of Aspen leaves

SUMMERTIME

God knows I've waited long enough
This dreary winter past
For any sign of summer
A daffodil, a blade of grass

Let me breathe the warm air once again
Feel the sun upon my back
Let me smell the scent of lilacs
See the melting streams come back

What a joy to be alive
To feel the sand between my toes
To run across the beach at night
And watch the tide as it comes and goes

You can have your winter skiing
The sledding and the mountain den
Let me have the summertime
Comes Spring, I'm born again

DREAMS

Dreams are but a thought we say
Reach out for them but too late
Upon awakening each new day
Our minds think back to recreate

When dreams across the crevice lie
Too far to reach, too deep, too wide
Think within those thoughts you hide
You'll find your dreams are wrapped inside

CROSSING BRIDGES

When you cross a bridge, you conquer a fault
One that's diminished the person you are
It's as if your life has come to a halt
To make yourself much better by far

Faults like anger, mistrust and belief
That have stopped you from growing in stature
When it happens it comes as a great relief
It feels like a form of rapture

So now that I'm in tune with myself
And have finally found the key
No longer I harbor those feelings I felt
I've crossed that bridge, you see

MYSTIC POWERS

I wondered many years ago
When discoveries of a kind
Would come from out of nowhere
Into my young mind

I thought that powers beyond belief
Were in complete control
That all the many joys of life
Were given to behold

And as the years went fleeting by
I then began to see
That all those mystic powers I sought
Were all a part of me

MOUNTAIN HIGH

They ask me why I like to hike
Up mountains that can humble
Where you strain to fill your lungs on high
And you sometimes trip and stumble

I like to go up to the mountain top
Where I can feel quite regal
I like to go up to the mountain top
Where my heart can soar like an eagle

TRAILERING

Let me roll along the highways
Watching life along the way
Through cities, towns and byways
Starlit nights and sunny days

Enjoying new places, people, things
Along the beaches and rolling hills
Cajun cooking, New England clamboils
Busy factories and textile mills

Meeting friends at every campground
Sharing stories, telling tales
Sitting by warming campfires
Driving through storms and windy gales

When day is done and campground nears
We roll on in and find a spot
Hook her up and chow on down
A loafer's life, it is not!

MORNING PRAYER

Protect me from tumultuous nights
And agonizing days
Save me from all greed and strife
And help me mend my ways

Protect me from the elements
And the problems over which I delve
But dear God most of all
Protect me from myself

DON'T TREAD ON ME

Don't trample on the flowers my friends
They yearn to live like you and I
And after we have passed it seems
They straighten up toward the sky

So as you hike along the fields
Watch where you step along your way
The flowers bend to stand aside
So they may live another day

We are all creatures on this earth
And share the space we treasure so
So when we're looking up ahead
We need to care where our feet go

Live foliage crops up everywhere
As among our friends we talk
Beware of all these litte souls
As we share the ground on which we walk

SAILING

Give me a ship that knows her way
Through stormy seas and skies so fair
Let out her sails to caress the winds
That plummet her forward for us who dare

Let her spinnaker ring with the song of gales
Across the stormy seas far and wide
As the waves lap at her bosom firm
And sweep along her sides

Let me take her 'round the horn again
To where my heart awaits
The clearing skies that urge me on
And stimulate my mates

So when the journey's end comes near
And homeward bound I gain
I'll look out toward the heavy seas
With plans to sail again

MILE HIGH CENTER

The Denver

ON REACHING SEVENTY

Here I am still standing up
I know my own name and who I am
Not feeble or frail or throwing up
Reached the point where I don't give a damn

In life we know its very little to give
As we all grow older along the way
Especially when considering the alternative
It's pretty damn nice I must say

You can go to bed late and still have a ball
And visit the grandest Bordello
But one of the best things that happens of all
Is to live anywhere in Colorado

Isn't it fun to just let things be
And gather to give nature its due
For the greatest treasure in life you see
Is to have friends exactly like you

Loving

HER BEAUTY LIES AWAKE

When once I felt her warm embrace
I yearned her not, 'twas not my place
Should I have been able to stay away
For just another day

Her beauty lies awake at night
And I in folly think it's me
That makes her sleepless time her plight
For thoughts she holds of me

How can we with our hearts on fire
Keep from the world our feelings held
While overwhelmed with great desire
With love so yearning felt

And if she in doubt the love I seek
I'll kneel and kiss her furrowed brow
That she should know of whom I speak
And hold in her bosom my heart for now

I walk along like one who dares
And think of places where she waits
And if just once she shows she cares
I'll wait however long it takes

SWEETHEARTS

When I was young and full of life
I'd walk along with pride
And carve a heart upon a tree
With both our names inside

One day when I am old and gray
I'll think of you and smile
As still I walk that same old trail
And sometimes stay awhile

THE SECRET OF LIFE

Come closer lest the world should hear
The secret of life I've found
That miracles do happen
Wherever life abounds

Some say it's wealth and power
Others claim it's liberty
Myself I thought for many years
It would never be known to me

I searched in books for knowledge
Hoping to find the key
To unlock the mysteries of life
For both you and me

It came at the most unexpected time
This gift for which I yearned
The secret of life as you will find
Is to love and be loved in return

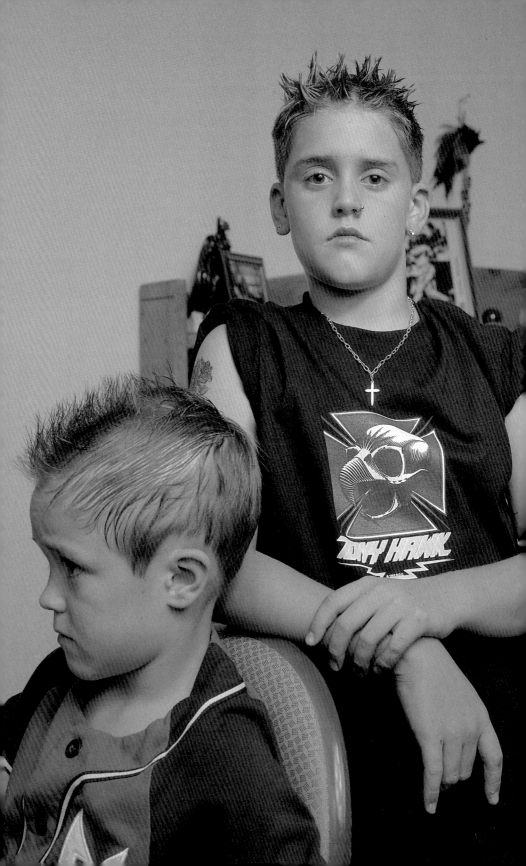

GRANDMA'S BOYS

I can see them playing there
The two little boys of Rose
Thinking thoughts of tomorrow
About what no one knows

And as the years kept passing by
A few little changes I'd see
The strange hairdos, earrings, and tattoos
Were driving me up a tree

What is happening to them I thought
Why can't they be just like me
It's just one of those facts of life
It's all in genetics you see

As I get on along the years
I can hear a voice from afar
"You must step back a few paces my dear
And love them the way that they are."

ETERNAL LOVE

When the stars have lost their glitter
And the moon has lost its glow
When earth's sweetness turns to bitter
And the summertime brings snow

When the waves no longer hammer
At the rocks and shores below
When the birds no longer sing their songs
And hobble to and fro

When dusk no longer follows dawn
And seagulls shun the shore
When fables fail to warm the heart
And dreamers dream no more

When lilacs fail to bloom again
And sea life fails to spawn
When children's laughter is no more
Will my love for you be gone

FIELD OF DREAMS

Through the fields where dreamers go
I'll be waiting for you there
And I want the world to know
I'll be searching everywhere

Till that day when we shall see
The place prepared for you and me
Where bluebirds flying overhead
Sing their songs and once was said
Life began there long ago
Even before I loved you so

When you finally do appear
I'll take hold of you my dear
And our hearts shall beat as one
Then I'll know my search is done

Though the storm clouds overhead
Cast their shadows over me
I'll keep looking through the fields
Where dreamers go, there I'll be

MOTHER

I can still see her sitting there
Curled up in her rocking chair
Her small hands moving to and fro
Making what I did not know

Hankies, cases, quilts abound
Now we have them all around
I used to wonder why the pace
To fill in each and every space

Her talents now have since long gone
And she's moved on to her reward
Now they're out there for all to see
She's calling out remember me

I guess we all would like to be
A part of someone's memory
It must be true as you can see
Is that why I write poetry?

IMAGES

Across the miles I often see
Images of you and me
The times we spent alone at last
The dreams we shared, the years long past

The way I always held your hand
When walking side by side
The warmth I felt from day to day
And thought of you with pride

When memories come back to me
And I recall your pleasant smile
I think it no disgrace at all
To weep awhile

THE JOURNEY

I walk down where the creek flows by
And the rocks crowd along the shore
Where the breezes blow and branches bend
And the leaves turn asking for more

Along the path that lilacs shade
Where the Aspen in Autumn turns bare
Over the hill where dreams are born
Someone waits for me there

BEYOND THE MIND

You hold their hands and walk them now
Your loved ones who now grasp you near
Their lives are passing you know not how
They live with doubt, they live with fear

It is we who have, who now must give
To those on others reliance seek
Our minds are clear, our bodies live
Their thinking gone, their bodies weak

When they upon your strength rely
And their survival is your lot
When contact fails as you try and try
Reach past their mind and touch their heart

AS TIME GOES BY

I like to think as time goes by
And you reminisce a time or two
That you sometimes have a thought of me
As I have a thought of you

There's nothing wrong in forgetting
As we live our daily lives
Living, loving and laughing
And saying hellos and goodbyes

But once we're done with our rituals
And there's nothing happening or new
Would you have a little thought about me
And I'll have a little thought about you

THINK OF ME

When your life is filled with memories
And your heart is filled with love
When you think about the years gone by
And those who have gone above

When you begin to feel the joy
Of Summer, Spring and Fall
When blossoms seem to meet your eyes
At every beck and call

When in your garden nature grows
Her beauty yours to see
While you embrace those whom you love
Will you sometimes think of me

LOVING YOU

Does it ever cross your mind
Of the love I have for you
Repeating it is just one way
Of letting you know I do
Together we've covered many miles
Hiding tears, showing smiles
Yet each day we try anew

LOVE LOST

Is it better to be alone
Than to be with me my love
And do a thousand things
You have not dreamed of

Is it better to be alone my dear
And toil at things for pleasure
Than feel the warmth of love
That we both treasure

And when the time does come
And you must say goodbye to strife
Will you then turn your head and say
Could I have better spent my life

Wait not until your body's cold
And left behind the one who cares
For when you reach there you will find
There is no love found there

DON'T ASK ME HOW I KNOW

She looked at me her hand in mine
When asked she put a kiss upon my cheek
I know that someday she will find
The peace she tried so hard to seek

Sometimes when I look there's nothing there
Though much is lost there are some gains
I somehow have become aware
Though the mind is gone the love remains

Somehow I know within the mind
Beneath the crevices below
There lies the love we seek to find
Don't ask me how I know, I know

A FRIEND

A friend is one who holds you dear
Through all your ups and downs
A friend loves you when you're happy
And when you're sad they frown

A friend is one who is honest
With you in every way
A friend will overlook your faults
And thinks of you day by day

A friend is one who is by your side
Through infirmities and strife
A friend will be there when needed
And for most a friend is for life

CAREGIVER

Long after God and healer turned resigned
We take what's left and lift the spirit high
That which remains will spend the day
In meaningless endeavor and ask not why

Our tasks are but to help along
Those souls who once were filled with life
Now empty we caress their shell
Our father, mother, husbands and wives

We feel no pity for ourselves
This burden we for now embrace
That those we loved will feel secure
For that short time that we must face

So as we must we'll carry on
And do whatever it will take
To use our strength to hold them high
And share together their unearned fate

So then when that sad task is done
And others who with burden bear
Need a hand to carry on
Ask a caregiver, they've been there

WORDS NOT SAID

I hope that I'm not one of those
Who looks back over life
And wishes that the words not said
Will haunt me like a knife

I want to tell you now my love
Before the time arrives
When memories become unclear
And we have spent our lives

How much you really mean to me
And of my love for you
So when I do come back again
I hope that you will too

As we have shared our love in life
And two grew into one
I loved you not only for what you are
But for what I have become

Let's take life for what it is
And live it hand in hand
The highs, the lows, the in betweens
A woman and her man

A ROSE

There's something about a rose
Its fragrance, its beauty
It stands as an example of what life
Should be, coming in many colors
Giving pleasure to others
As it stands proudly in defiance
Of all that is negative

Aging gracefully with each day
It opens widely and reveals its knowledge
As you bend to share its fragrance
And learn from its beauty

Even in death its beauty is not diminished
It bows gracefully and majestically
And its fragrance lingers
A rose

Leaving

YOUR SPIRIT WILL ENDURE

In life with strength you work to do your best
Meeting each challenge along the way
With pounding heart that beats within your breast
And pauses with each new coming day

In midlife as your stride begins to slow
Determined you double your resolve
With challenges that follow where you go
And in your mind they still revolve

The latter years are calm or so it seems
Compared to those that came before
And with them follow all your dreams
That push you on no more

When the end comes and it will you can be sure
And your heart has given all it has to give
Your spirit will prevail and still endure
In those who ever knew you lived

ON GROWING OLD

It's not the way I thought it would be
Growing old I mean
I thought I'd have another chance
But that was not to be

I'd wear my son's old cast-off shirts
A youthful style I thought
The size still fits, a great relief
Especially the ones I bought

I'd lie in the sun the whole day through
A healthy tan I'd aquire
I'd exercise and jog a mile
For everyone to admire

But when all was said and done
I still would have to face
The same old man I left behind
I just can't keep the pace

Oh well, I guess I've had my day
My friends agree and smile
Let youth go on and have their fling
I think I'll rest awhile

THE EARTH IS OURS

Fear not that journey's end is near
For those of us who've come this far
As you will all come soon to hear
It is the beginning of a new start

When dreams no longer fill your mind
And we contented then must be
With fantasies of days gone by
The way it used to be

Blessed are those whose time has come
To join with others as we all must
The earth is ours for us to roam
With our eternal dust

THERE YOU ARE

Let not the thought of your demise
Leave you trembling with fear
For we are but a link in the chain of life
And wherever you go it is clear

From man to dust to fertile land
To flowers and fauna we leave behind
From wildlife, forest and ocean sands
And spawning life of every kind

To be one again with nature
Do you think this life we'll miss
This could be our greatest treasure
Being part of this eternal bliss

Find a lilac in full bloom
With its fragrance from afar
Look inside its small cocoon
There you are.

HELL NO

They lied to me before I came
They said that Hell was a pleasure
That it was mostly fun and games
And most of it I'd treasure

It was a deception from the start
The stories I was told
That the flames were only one foot high
And the floors were actually cold

It was all new to me of course
The screams and yells from the burning
Most of them were on barbecue spits
And like shishkebab were turning

I stood in line with all the rest
Getting our supplies from the devil
He said that the coal was replaced with oil
Then gave me a pick and a shovel

THE CHAIN OF LIFE

Are we but a link in the chain of life
Whether the beginning or end we do not know
We share dreams with others, love and strife
Sitting and wondering, wherever we go

Starting with soil that nourishes all
Plants that feed animals and ourselves too
We watch this through winter, summer and fall
With each new morning it starts anew

The flowers the grasses and beauty of life
High hilltops and mountains that startle our senses
We spend a lifetime just asking why
As we gather and gossip over white picket fences

The rivers and streams that flow through our lives
Looking up at the stars, sun, clouds and the moon
And bees that make condos out of their hives
That we must leave, all but too soon

We are here for a short time before bidding goodbye
Searching eternally to find the lost key
It's here for the asking if you will but try
We are a link in the food chain, you see

DEPARTED

I hope that you're not crying
Your tears always saddened me
I know this must seem like forever
And your sorrow will always be

Not so, just take my word for it
Have faith and soon you'll see
I've just gone on to pay respects
To friends and family

They say that life is a pathway
Between two eternities
If you now think that life is great
Wait till you follow me

SEARCH ON NO MORE

As we wander through life enjoying the view
The mountains, the blossoms and sunsets galore
And we know from the past there's nothing that's new
Those that precede us have seen it before

How much of your time have you spent in this life
Trying to contemplate all that it means
Living and dying and in between strife
Too much thought given this, or so it seems

We watch with amazement as people pass by
Are they too in wonder asking everyone why
Is there a reason, it's too close to call
We're here for a short time, then not at all

Where comes this beauty, just look past the door
Ashes at first, then to dust
Search on no more
It is us!

LIFE

Ah life it is so fleeting
It seems like yesterday I ran
In open fields with children meeting
And traversing across the land

And now the twilight years are here
So I contemplate about my youth
And watch the end approaching near
As in aging horses, long in tooth

It's strange but no sadness do I feel
I've had many good years to dream
And many wounds I've had to heal
But more good times than bad it seems

I've enjoyed this life and shed no tears
And to know you all was my gain
Hope I did not miss you while I was here
For I shall not pass this way again

HELLO AGAIN

They came to me those souls from the past
Mostly when I was lonely for their presence
They had gone when I was not there to say goodbye
A void remains but they left their essence

I look to the day when we shall be one again
When our spirits will be together and go on from there
For there is no doubt that we are all one with nature
And this long journey is ours to share

For it is our destiny to return from whence we came
To repay the debt to those who gave us life
That others may take our place
So we may leave behind our heartaches and strife
And move on to eternity

MY GIFT

They were all gifted our three
The oldest attractive and bright
Our youngest born to create
The middle one a shining light

Each went their own special way
Busy living their lives
The oldest had the most to say
She certainly earned the right

The youngest was destined to heal
And made medicine his primary goal
Understanding, tenderness and people
Were all part of his mold

The son between them had planned
To leave his mark on life
He struggled to make his stand
And tried with all his might

As we look back now at their lives
We are proud how they all fared
It was the middle one who said
Dad, why am I running so scared
Then one day too soon he was gone
Long before his time
His struggle had taken its toll
God, would that it were mine

As they came to pay their respects
All those whose life he had shared
I could hear his voice in the night
That was my gift Dad, I cared

GOODBYE MY LOVE

Let me hold you in my arms
Once more before you turn cold
Let me feel your warm embrace
I won't release my hold

May your journey be a great one
I'll get along somehow
Take my heart with you
I have no need for it now

ETERNAL GARDENS

I walked along the stones one day
Saw monuments by those who cared
Touched flowers that were standing guard
It was so tranquil there

There were monuments that touched the sky
Alongside those scarcely seen
As if it mattered where you lie
Along the green

The larger ones were shouting out
Here I am you mortals there
The little ones would look askance
And proudly used their shade

In a hundred years who will care
Who lies beneath this sod of grass
Scatter my dust along the trail
Where deer and hikers pass

MOURN NOT MY PASSING

Mourn not my passing, I was ready
Not like some
Who linger on past their time
Before they come

Life was a pleasure to me
I drank of its full measure
No regrets, just love for those I left behind
Family and friends were my greatest treasure

I should have known my time had come
When I looked up and found
The sun, the stars, the earth and I
And Universe were one

Let's journey on together
It's not so different here
The ones that went before us gather
To hold us near

The endless time, the beauty here
For all of us to see
Come share with me this treasure
For all eternity

WHY

I lied when I said I was ready
I never was you know
I wanted to live a thousand years
I never wanted to go

Oh why did he make the sky so blue
The snow white clouds above
Why did he put the mountains there
And send you for me to love

Why did he make the ocean waves
That always beckoned me
Why did he make this life so rare
Then insist that I must leave

A TIME TO LIVE

It surprises me to this day
The grief that still abounds
When a loved one passes on
The crying and awful sounds

We all seem to miss the point
That dying is not a choice
But a journey that we do anoint
And something to rejoice

Pushing up Daisies, they used to say
Do you know what that really means
No, not on our backs with arms held up
But nourishing them with our genes

We forget sometimes our role in life
As obvious as it seems
It's to help those who follow us
And relish all their dreams

There is a time to live
And a time to die
We should understand the reason
Both you and I

LONG NOT

Long not for those who leave us now
To make their peace with God
Our hearts are never far apart
Although it seems so hard

Ask not what life is all about
We never know for sure
We only know for those we love
Our feelings will endure

And as the years go fleeting by
You'll find it all too true
They've only gone ahead you see
To make a place for you

THE LONG GOODBYE

She knows she's dying
And I am crying
It's not for trying
To bring her back

She played no role
In growing old
And turning cold
With love not lacked

There is no reason
In any season
Just short of treason
To make me pack

I cannot leave her
And still I grieve her
She knows I need her
And that's a fact

This life of mine
Is not worth a dime
Until the time
I work through that

My tears are flowing
And I am growing
Fearful of knowing
No turning back

I'll hold her closely
And kiss her mostly
She'll look quite ghostly
And turn her back

Let her go now
She'll show you how
She'll turn and vow
To say goodbye